Running Shoes

CAROLE SANEK

GWN Publishing, LLC

Published by: GWN Publishing
www.GWNPublishing.com

Cover Design: Kristina Conatser

ISBN: 978-1-965971-26-0

For every survivor who believed they couldn't leave.
This is proof that you can.

Contents

The Shoes I Wore

No one who stood outside my life ever understood my why. They didn't feel the fire that surged in my chest, the pressure of staying when it meant disappearing entirely. They weren't there when survival meant walking through fire, when the walls were closing in, and I could either burn or find a way out.

I didn't walk away from my children. I walked away from a house full of ghosts—echoes of past choices that threatened to consume us all. I walked toward something raw and uncertain: hope. And through it all, I carried Lexie with me.

I already knew about Thom and the HIV diagnosis. It wasn't a shock—both he and my brother were battling the same fight, one that had already taken too much. But when the call came, there was no hesitation. Thom's voice, though fading, still carried the weight of a life lived with brilliance and wild light. I couldn't ignore it any longer. I packed my car and stepped into the unknown, knowing that this was the one thing my brother would have wanted me to do. To choose action over waiting, to keep moving toward the light, even when it was dimming faster than I could bear. Staying would cost me everything. But leaving, I realized, was what I had to do.

You can judge my distance. You can measure my motherhood by your standards, but not a single one of you stood in my shoes.

My shoes were blistered. Torn. They'd walked through grief, through the kind of survival that takes everything from you, and sacrifice so deep it carved me into someone new.

But those shoes never walked away from love—not once.

This book isn't about proving myself. It's about telling the truth—the raw truth. The kind most people refuse to hear. But here it is anyway.

I didn't abandon. I adapted. I didn't quit. I chose to live, and in doing so, I gave my daughter a chance to do the same.

So before you turn the page, ready to judge, take a breath. Because you're about to understand what it truly takes to run in shoes like mine.

Why We Run

Traumatized people don't run because they're reckless. We run because staying feels like suffocating in slow motion, like drowning beneath the weight of everything we cannot change. The air becomes thick with memories that grip you like chains, and survival, at times, means breaking free.

We run not to abandon. We run to breathe. To reclaim ourselves. To find the space to heal and remember who we are, without the weight of the bruises and scars that linger.

Sometimes, we run *toward* something better—something we can't yet see, but feel deep inside. Even when we don't know the way, even when the pain cuts deeper than we ever imagined, we run.

Running isn't a weakness. It's instinct. It's the body's whisper, urgent and raw: *Move. Or you won't survive.*

Chapter One

Running Toward Chicago

The Years of Rebirth, 1988–1990

I didn't stumble into survival. I clawed my way here, barefoot, bleeding, fire at my back and silence ahead. The world called it strength. I called it stubborn breath. And still, somehow, there were butterflies—even in the ash, even when I didn't deserve beauty, they landed. That's the truth: I didn't find grace. Grace found me.

***

Chicago wasn't just a city I chose—it was the one I'd been running toward my entire life. As a child, I'd whispered to my parents that someday I'd live there, and years later, I made it happen. It was close enough to Cleveland to return if I had to, but far enough away to finally breathe, to exhale a freedom I hadn't known I needed.

I found the apartment on a weekend trip—a place for Lexie, me, and the two cats. It wasn't fancy, but it was ours. After years of living life on someone else's terms, that mattered more than anything. But even with new walls and a fresh key, the old ghosts came with us. You can't shake off years of control in a single U-Haul ride.

I called in favors, packed the remnants of my life, loaded the U-Haul, hitched my car—and we were gone. Lexie stayed behind to finish her school year, leaving me—just me—alone in the city I'd always dreamed of, with nothing but time and silence to fill.

I unpacked. I worked. I helped the cats adjust. I told myself I was fine. Fine. It was the word I used when I didn't want to admit that I was still raw, still breaking, still searching for pieces of myself I hadn't known I lost. Fine was what I said when I didn't want Lexie to see the cracks.

But the truth? I wasn't just moving into an apartment. I was stepping into the unknown, carrying more baggage than the boxes we unloaded.

I wasn't walking away—I was running. Not jogging, not walking—running. Because it was the only way I knew how to escape the past that clung to me like a second skin.

Soon, I had some lovely friends, and Lexie was finding her way too. The apartment had a private entry in the back, giving her freedom she never abused. It was all about giving her something different—something better.

We spent weekends discovering the city, the vibrancy of it, the life pulsing through the streets. And on those beautiful days, when the city sparkled and the sun warmed the pavement, I'd tell Lexie, "Look for the Sears Tower." I wanted her to always know her way home. But what I didn't tell her was that I wasn't just showing her Chicago. I was trying to show her a life that didn't feel broken. I wanted her compass to point toward something more than just the Sears Tower.

Our apartment was just a mile and a half from downtown, nestled in a vibrant neighborhood that had a little bit of everything—glamour, grit, and everything in between. Movies had been filmed here, TV shows written about the neighborhood. It was diverse, gritty, and yes, it had its problems. But when we closed our door at night, we had our own slice of safety and glamour—until the night the front door of the building was stolen. And the night robbers broke into our landlord's unit while he was home. He was knocked out of the bathroom window, fell to the first floor, and got trapped. The police had to remove him from the basement. That window, the one we'd thought was just a window, served no real purpose.

Lexie worked at the local grocery store, and later at a country club, where she was often hired to babysit the members' children. She was making her own money, building her own world. I was back in the world of cancer treatment, working at a cancer center. It felt like a lifetime ago that I'd trained in Los Angeles for this new job, learning to operate a device designed to kill cancer cells by microwaving them. No one was ever harmed, as physicists calculated the exact dosage needed for each treatment.

Our second year in Chicago began with Lexie starting her senior year of high school. I was sent to a conference in Las Vegas, and though it should've been uneventful, it became yet another crack in the fragile life I was clinging to. But the truth is, I was always waiting for the other shoe to drop. Trauma had trained me to look for cracks in the sidewalk, even on sunny days.

I was walking through the casino toward the meeting rooms when I was knocked to the ground, my purse stolen. Just like that, I had no ID, no credit cards, no cash—and in one of the dumbest moves I've ever made, I had left my car keys in the purse instead of the hotel safe.

The hotel staff was gracious, arranging for American Express to rush me a new card, but my keys were gone. My purse eventually turned up in a trash can with my ID still inside—but the keys? Gone. I called home right away, had our landlord change the locks, and then started calling the man I was seeing. He had a spare key to my car.

I tried for three days. He never answered.

In desperation, I even called the hotel manager in Macon, Virginia. That's when I found out he wasn't there. He wasn't anywhere he said he was.

Eventually, they tracked him down. He still had time to get the key to the airline, but he didn't. He dropped it off after I was already home.

I had trusted him, but he simply didn't care.

While I was still at the conference—shaken, but determined to finish what I came for—I met a man over dinner who owned a company that manufactured ultrasound hyperthermia devices used to treat cancer.

Somewhere between the clink of glasses and polite conversation, he asked if I'd ever consider becoming the company's Clinical Application Specialist. Without hesitation, I said yes. The only catch? The company was two hours outside of Chicago. It meant moving again.

But Lexie was ready for a fresh start. She graduated in June, and by July, we were gone.

We threw a party to celebrate her graduation—my brother, my mother, and Adam all came. It was one of those rare nights when everything felt almost right. Laughter, toasts, the city twinkling behind us.

If I'd known it would be the last time I'd see my brother, I would have begged him to stay. To stay forever. Danny had this way about him—a mischievous grin, eyes that always held the punchline of some dirty joke he wasn't telling.

I never imagined he had less than two years left to live. Dammit. He wasn't supposed to leave me with Mom. He wasn't supposed to leave me to grow old without him.

My father. The children's father. Now my brother. All the men I loved...gone. Leaving me to fight the good fight of life alone. And so I kept running—because sometimes, it's all you know how to do.

Chapter Two

Running, Flying

1990–1991

After telling my cheating boyfriend I was leaving, I spent weekends running to Champaign—a small town with nothing but corn, cows, and a whole lot of nothing else. Running from him. Running from the life that almost broke me.

The new opportunity was exciting—lots of travel to familiar cities, and others I couldn't wait to explore. But what I didn't realize was that I was still running. I wasn't just looking for new places to visit; I was searching for new ground to stand on—somewhere I wouldn't be haunted by the past, or by the choices I'd made to survive.

The move went smoothly, and my first exposure to what I was hired to do was to drive back to Chicago and attend a meeting of physicists who all worked in the field of ultrasound technologies. I sat through this meeting of minds, not quite sure what to expect, but I was welcomed warmly. After all, this was a male-dominated industry, and there I was, a woman—a fish out of water.

On my way home, I exited the Dan Ryan Expressway and stopped for gas near the Sears Tower. I will always call it that—I eventually married a man who was the project manager for its construction. The name is etched in my heart.

While pumping gas, a gust of Chicago wind ripped through, unwrapping my silk dress like it was a joke. There I was, at a gas station, silk dress gone rogue, standing in my black bra and panties, clutching at fabric like it could save me. A man at the next pump grinned and asked, "Do you come here often?" I laughed it off later, but in the moment, the exposure wasn't just fabric — it was the fear of being stripped bare in every sense.

That was my first day on the job.

Time passed, and Lexie and I fell into a rhythm. She worked at the local grocery store, figuring out what came next. I was flying all over the country—most trips over weekends—wining and dining hospital executives and radiology physicians.

The weeks blurred into boarding passes and hotel keys. I couldn't tell you if it was spring or fall—my life was measured in departure gates. Constant motion was its own disguise. If I never stopped moving, maybe the past wouldn't catch up. Maybe I wouldn't have to stop long enough to feel it.

Somewhere between all that running and flying, I hit a cow. Literally. Outside Champaign, I came around a bend and there she was, standing in the road like she owned it. I braked, she mooed, and I clipped her backside. She was fine—gave me side-eye and trotted off—but my nerves weren't. Turns out the farmer's fence had broken, and he tried to sue the company. Me? I still made the flight. I always made the flight. I joked about it — hitting a cow—but the truth is, I was always braced for impact. Trauma had trained me to expect collisions, no matter how unlikely.

Not every trip ended with laughter. Miami was proof of that. It was the city where fun cracked open into trauma—and it started with one night I'll never forget.

We were in town for a trade show and my favorite saleswoman was with us, and since we did not get to see each other very often, we partied. The last night after a closing dinner we grabbed one of our favorite strait-laced PhD's, and off we went down to Bayfront, the hot spot in Miami. We could walk there, our hotel was close.

After we had partied there our favorite PhD suggested we walk back to our hotel. We had to walk through a park-like atmosphere with dark bushes along the sidewalk. As we walked we were laughing and carrying on when our PhD said, "Do not turn around, do not look at me now, keep walking to the hotel."

The laughter died in my throat. His voice wasn't playful — it was sharp, clipped, like steel. My stomach dropped. I didn't dare ask why.

He was actually my boss and I knew his work history, including the fact that he could speak multiple languages. He had been on a ship in the China Sea during the Vietnam War "listening" to conversations. And I was pretty sure he had a government job.

We got to the hotel and went immediately to the bar where we could see the front door, and when he walked in, we had immediate relief. We all took a table, and I admit by then Susan and I were shaken. Then he told the story in one sentence: "He had a knife."

Three words. That's all he gave us. The bar noise clattered on around us, but for me, time froze. Some truths don't need details—they only need the chill that settles in your bones.

There were no reports the next morning of anyone found lying in that park, and we all went to the airport. The memory followed me onto the plane. Miami had left its mark, whether anyone else saw it or not.

Not all tradeshows and conferences ended badly. In Philadelphia, I was sitting with my favorite physicists when I heard a familiar voice—Tony Bennett. A server confirmed he was singing at a benefit one floor up. I nudged my favorite PhD, leaned in close, and whispered, "Come with me." The words slipped out like a challenge, laced with a spark that neither of us could ignore.

We snuck through the kitchen, took the service elevator, and there he was in full tuxedoed glory. We stayed in the back of the room, soaking it in. When he finished "I Left My Heart In San Francisco," we slipped back unnoticed. Every time I saw that PhD after, we shared a quiet toast with bourbon, our eyes locking over the rim of our glasses. The lines blurred, and for the first time in decades, I felt something I hadn't in so long—wanted, free. No expectations. No apologies. Just the heat of the moment, and the space between us where nothing needed to be said.

This was freedom. I had married at 18 and left at 42. Acting like a crazed teenager was in my blood again.

I had teenage crushes before I was married. I saw the Beatles, the Rolling Stones. My friend and I tried to sneak into the Stones' dressing room once. A security guard offered entry for a crude favor. Not knowing who was supposed to pay that price, we ran. He was too overweight to catch us. Inside, the band assumed we were groupies sent by a radio station. We were virgins. That wasn't the plan. We bolted again. And I've seen women older than me throw panties at Tom Jones. So, there.

Time raced on. I traveled to Los Angeles, San Francisco, Albuquerque, Dallas, Philadelphia, Detroit, Columbus, Pittsburgh, Milwaukee, Chicago, Indianapolis, and all over Illinois. I taught physicians and technicians how to use our equipment—still under FDA pre-market approval. I poured myself into the work, because work asked nothing personal of me. No confessions. No truths. Just the version of me who could smile, teach, and disappear.

Lexie and I made trips back to Chicago for special occasions. One Christmas, I gave her tickets to see "The Phantom of the Opera."

Freedom came with wild stories. In LA, we took PhDs to dinner at a famous restaurant. The company AmEx was declined because money in a research environment is tight and depends on grants. The scientists pooled their personal cards. I knew we had two issues left: the hotel and the rental van.

We formed a plan. I told everyone to leave the hotel through a side entrance the next morning. I drove us to LAX, told them to get out at the terminal, and handed the van keys to a valet. My team thought we were committing a crime. Over coffee, I said, "We're not the first. We won't be the last."

The worst part? A $100 retrieval fee. Pocket change for freedom.

I wasn't practicing to land behind bars. I just needed to get home.

I often stood in front of the mirror, not recognizing the woman staring back. For the first time in decades, I wasn't someone's daughter, wife, or mother. I was just... me. The heroine, not the victim. The woman in the mirror wasn't the girl who survived, or the wife who endured. She was someone else entirely—a stranger I was still learning to trust.

Another adventure: Detroit. My boss and I were stuck in traffic on the way to the airport. Last flight out. I looked at him. He looked at me. I said, "Buckle up, buttercup."

We left the car on the ramp. Another $100 fee.

In July, it ended. I was laid off. Lexie had moved to Texas with her boyfriend. I was out of work and not thrilled about staying in Champaign.

I called a former supervisor in Chicago. In five minutes, I had a new job in Richmond, Virginia. I was on the run again.

There were sad goodbyes. Too much fun to call it work. I had treated two celebrities, met President Reagan when he cut the ribbon on a new machine in Santa Monica.

The road was calling again.

Time to lace up my running shoes once more.

Chapter Three

Bouncing Between Grief and New Beginnings

I had just finished a year of bouncing—the kind that rattles your bones, like when a flight hits an air pocket and makes you question if you'll land safely at all.

Then there was the bouncing of the rental truck, hauling me and my life from Illinois to Virginia, through the mountains, with a cat beside me who was losing her breakfast thanks to the tranquilizer I'd given her.

Miss Scarlett was my cat's name. She'd lived in Cleveland, Chicago, and Champaign. We were now leaving the "C" cities behind to start over in the South, where strangers said hello and vowels stretched out like lazy summer afternoons.

I had already flown to Richmond to finalize an apartment, to get a feel for the area, and meet the CFO of the hospital where I'd be working. I liked everything I saw.

I chose a charming neighborhood called The Fan. It was near the art museum, not far from a speedway that roared to life on summer nights, and just a few blocks from downtown.

I was blessed—good friends from Chicago and beyond looked out for me. They arranged for someone to help unload the truck.

When I pulled up in front of my new place, he was waiting. I got the car off the trailer, lifted the truck's door, and when it was all done, I collapsed onto a futon, body aching, heart full.

I started a new job at a large hospital, hired to meet with insurance companies who were denying claims until full audits were done. My job? Prove the bills were legitimate. And I was good—really good.

I'd done this in Cleveland and Chicago. I enjoyed being on the hospital's side, especially because most of the time, the errors favored them. I won almost every case. I even had a national reputation for being sharp. It felt good to be known for something that mattered.

Then came August. The phone rang as I opened the front door.

It was my brother.

He was calling from Amsterdam. He had made the decision to go to the hospital for physician-assisted suicide. I crumpled to the floor. The word suicide didn't belong in the same breath as my brother's name. My brain tried to reject it, like oil refusing to mix with water.

My baby brother. My Itchy Brother. He needed our mother by his side.

She was living in a memory care facility. I had to make sure her passport was valid, arrange for a car to take her to the airport, and ensure someone at JFK would help her board her flight to Amsterdam.

Danny promised to handle everything once she arrived—and he did. Like a boss.

His friends took her to dinner, walked with her, sat outside his hospital room when he passed. She stayed another week, scattered his ashes in a favorite park, then flew home.

And I resumed the responsibility of keeping her safe.

I remember her visiting Lexie and me in Chicago. She'd walk to McDonald's for a Filet-O-Fish, and she'd sell her cigarettes to the homeless people for $1 each.

She never paid for her sandwich.

When I told that story to Danny at Lexie's graduation party, he laughed so hard he leaned back in his chair, roaring. It's one of the last memories I have of him so full of life.

After we lost him, the world kept moving—leaves turned, winds shifted. Grief is cruel that way—it doesn't pause the seasons. The world spins on, even when yours has shattered.

Fall came.

In Virginia, it looked a lot like the Midwest—same golden trees, same chill in the air. But everything felt different.

Through work, I met a man—an attorney named Edward. We started dating.

He was a die-hard Virginia Tech fan, which meant weekends often revolved around football games in Blacksburg. He bled orange and maroon.

By Christmas, I'd met his family. I watched them exchange gifts—and was mystified to learn they ironed their wrapping paper and reused it. I questioned him on the way home. He brushed it off as tradition. I called it weird. But it was these little glimpses into his world that made me realize how different we were—how much I was stepping into something unfamiliar.

He was sober. His brother too. He'd been sober for years. Should that have been a red flag? Maybe.

Still, we spent weekends together. I met his neighbors. I cooked, he cleaned up. We threw parties. Life felt lighter, the kind of lighter that came with intimacy that wasn't just physical, but a connection that kept the world at bay.

But he was fun. I still had a drink here and there, but I respected his space. It worked.

That fall, one of his close friends from England came to visit for Guy Fawkes Day. His name was Bertie.

He was charming, proper, and polite—and it felt damn good to have another man on my arm for a change. He was the bee's knees.

Edward, himself was well-traveled. He had three degrees and had passed the bar in two states plus D.C. He still wore his letter sweater and saddle shoes to reunions. He was a character.

That spring, he surprised me with a trip to England. Bertie would show us around.

It was March—cold, damp—but I slapped on a lipstick smile, boarded trains, hailed taxis. I nearly jumped out of my skin when a cherry bomb went off in Trafalgar Square. The IRA lived in the back of my mind.

We ate scones with clotted cream. I learned to love fish and chips. I explored castles and wandered green countryside I didn't know could exist.

And in those moments… I started noticing flashes of anger. Over little things.

I told myself he was tired. Stressed. Jet-lagged. That's all.

We said goodbye to Bertie and headed north to Edinburgh.

I am Clan Gordon. I did not want to leave. That city felt like art to me—so beautifully layered I wanted to drink it in.

We visited a friend near Aberdeen. I helped deliver a calf. Edward left the barn.

I was in love—with Scotland.

Back in the States, I went to find my purse one evening and realized it was gone.

The screen on my back door had been slashed. Someone had broken in.

It was Friday. I spent the evening canceling cards and making DMV appointments.

Edward showed up with boxes.

"Come on," he said. "You're not staying here. We'll pack this weekend and have a company get the rest."

That kind of extreme kindness meant the world. It felt like rescue. But rescue has a way of disguising chains.

So I moved in. A five-bedroom house and an acre of land.

And everything I owned?

It went into his attic.

Looking back now, I can see it. That was the day I started to lose myself.

The day everything I owned disappeared into an attic was the day I stopped running. I thought I'd landed somewhere safe.

But the truth is... I was still bouncing. The attic wasn't just where my boxes went. It was where my identity started to collect dust.

I just didn't know it yet.

Chapter Four

Rebound

Starting Over in Richmond

When Edward moved me into his home, I found myself on the edge of town, far from everything I'd known. It felt like I was slipping further from the life I thought I wanted. The city limits mirrored my isolation, and soon, I knew it was time to find work closer to home.

I spotted an ad for a nurse/auditor position with a large healthcare company. It wasn't just a job; it felt like a lifeline—something that could pull me back into the world I'd been retreating from. The salary was good, and the promise of floating between two hospitals on the south side of the city gave me structure, even if it felt like a distraction at first.

I loved the work. I was good at it. I was soon promoted to senior nurse auditor and began flying to different states as needed to verify charges for insurance companies. This is how for-profit organizations secure payments owed to them. Edward liked to joke I was the "attorney of record" for the company because of my negotiating skills.

But there were signs of tension at home. Moments where things could snap. I learned to tiptoe around the triggers, mastering the art of silence. One day, while cleaning the kitchen cupboards, I found a grocery bag filled with broken coffee mugs.

Edward had collected mugs from his travels—tiny relics of places he'd been, lives he'd lived. The story behind them shook me. He told me his former girlfriend had smashed them when they broke up. He had kept the shattered pieces. Who keeps shattered pieces of the past? Someone who hasn't let go. Someone who wants the reminder sharp enough to cut. I offered to fix them, and we brought them to a repair shop. At least then, he could look at them without flinching.

There was so much anger in that house—not just his. Mine, too. I decided then: silence was safer. Silence became my armor. But armor, worn too long, sinks into your skin.

The new job brought some relief. I was flying often—sometimes twice a week. Each flight felt like a breath of air away from the tension I lived in. Airports became my therapy rooms. Boarding passes, my prescriptions. Motion was the only medicine that worked. Mondays meant escape. Fridays meant return. I didn't miss the guilt of leaving. I welcomed the space.

Edward, of course, wasn't thrilled. He made sure I paid half the household bills, plus food and utilities. And because I was gone so much, he insisted I pay for a cleaning lady—since the one cleaning lady (me) was now airborne most weeks.

Atlanta became a regular stop. I worked with auditors buried in backlogs. Dinner alone at the bar became my routine—silent, with the hum of nearby conversations fading into background noise. Some nights, I'd sit at the pool in my robe, dip my feet into the water, then slip beneath its surface. Floating, weightless, was the only peace I could find. It was a quiet escape from the tension that followed me home, where I was never really alone.

Then there was the week I *wasn't* alone. I met him over dinner, and for that week, I was never alone in the pool. The water, the intimacy, the way his presence filled the space—it was the first time in a long while I felt like I could breathe freely, fully.

Dallas. Houston. Repeat. In Houston, I always made time for Lexie. She was thriving, and we'd meet for dinner or I'd stay at her place. I treasured those moments. They grounded me.

Despite the travel, I felt isolated. No close friends. No confidantes. Just Edward, three cats, and soon—a Lovebird.

Edward thought I needed a pet. He bought me a bird. Winston. The thing was pure hell. He bit me—hard. Not a peck, a full-on attack. Edward, naturally, adored him. Let him nap in his shirt pocket. I, meanwhile, was nursing puncture wounds.

Then came Hokie—a young Moluccan Cockatoo. Bigger bird. Bigger responsibility. And this one loved me. He'd lie upside down in my arms like a baby. It made Edward jealous.

Not long after, Edward took a solo trip to London. I didn't think much of it. He had old friends there. Unfinished business, he said. Then a letter showed up—carelessly left on his desk. A note from an old flame. I confronted him. He brushed it off, quick with his lawyerly tongue. I didn't push. I folded that betrayal into the growing box I kept hidden—the one filled with the betrayals that came in many forms: broken promises, slammed doors, silent nights after storms.

Earlier that year, Edward had proposed a getaway to the Florida Keys—a return to the place where he had once lived, once partied, once practiced law. What he really wanted, I realize now, was to chase down the man he used to be.

The trip started badly. The day before we left, Edward lost his briefcase—wallet and all. So I paid for everything. Flights. Hotels. Meals.

At the Palm Beach airport, he threw a fit at security and was kicked out. I had to rent the car and drive us to the Keys while he sulked beside me.

The trip was nothing like the fantasy he sold me. The Keys were beautiful. Edward was not. He was moody, bitter, far from the man I thought I knew.

Later that year, we flew to Maui to visit his daughter. Paradise couldn't save us. We argued. Loudly. Hotel security was called. Strangers recoiled. There's nothing lonelier than being screamed at in paradise. The ocean roared, but all I heard was shame.

We stayed the week, smiled for his daughter, pretended. But something inside me cracked. I couldn't ignore the truth anymore.

Life continued. We went through motions. Then came autumn of 1993—and everything cracked.

Back home, I slipped back into routine. Work. Travel. Silence. Then, one morning, I remembered I hadn't had a mammogram in almost two years.

I saw a poster at one of the hospitals offering Saturday mammograms. Bright. Cheerful. Too cheerful. I booked an appointment. Just something to check off the list. But the thing about lists is they can turn on you. Sometimes the box you check holds the truth you've been running from.

That Saturday, I went in. The tech smiled and said, "See you next year."

"Maybe sooner," I replied. I don't know why I said it. I just knew.

The following week, I was in Atlanta. I checked messages from my hotel. My doctor's voice was on the machine. Calm. Too calm. I needed a biopsy. Urgently.

I ran to my car and screamed. Then I booked the earliest flight home.

Edward met me at the airport. Not alone. He brought Katherine—his best friend's wife. The woman he often said he should have married.

He didn't want a scene. He knew I'd be crying. So, he came with emotional insulation. I sat silently on the drive home, tears in my eyes.

The following week was a blur. I saw the surgeon. Guide wire. Mammograph-guided biopsy. Local anesthetic.

"Eighty percent of patients with microcalcifications don't have cancer," he said.

I looked him in the eye. "Just call me the lucky twenty."

I knew.

Friday. 3:30 PM. The call came.

"Mrs. Hunter, the biopsy results are back. You have ductal carcinoma in situ. You do have breast cancer."

I couldn't process the rest. Just those words. Breast cancer.

The words clanged in my head like a bell that wouldn't stop ringing. Breast cancer. My name stitched to a sentence I never wanted.

I sat at the window, watching Edward mow the back forty, tears streaming down my face.

I was certain I was going to die.

Chapter Five

Pink is NOT My Color

October 1993

I sat at the dining room table, while outside Edward carved circles into the lawn with the riding mower like he was cutting a masterpiece. I could see the sweat running down his face as he went around and around, and I sat there with tears running down mine. The smell of gasoline wafted in, and I closed the sliding door.

It felt like parody—life going in circles outside, while mine had just slammed into a wall.

Then I looked at the clock and realized it was still a working day in California. I ran to find my address book and the private number of an oncologist

I had worked with several years before. I sat there, praying he would answer, and suddenly his voice said, "Hello, Carole, are you calling to check on your machine?"

I bit my lip, my voice shaking. I told him the news. I heard him take a deep breath and then say, "From what you're telling me, this is a tiny cancer, the size of a pea. See your surgeon next week. He'll give you the full report. Get a copy and send it to me—here's my fax number."

His calm steadied me like a rope tossed into deep water. But when I put the phone down, the silence in that house roared back louder than ever.

He was right: it was tiny. But when you hear the words, "You have cancer," you hit the floor. You see yourself wasting away.

Edward finally finished the grass and came through the garage. I turned from the table. He took one look at my face and asked, "What's wrong, baby?"

I let it all fall from my lips—everything I knew—and he stood there stunned. He reminded me we would see the surgeon together the following week, then went to take a shower. Yeah, he wasn't a very emotional man.

I washed my face, put on lipstick, and left for the grocery store. Life was still moving forward. Dinner had to be made.

I parked and walked in. To this day, I remember feeling like my life was spinning at 33⅓ RPM while everyone else was spinning at 78. My feet felt heavy. Every step took effort. It was as if I'd fallen out of my own body. I wanted to scream, "How do you people not know I have breast cancer?" But nobody knew. Nobody seemed to care. I was invisible in the checkout line, carrying a secret that felt heavier than the cart itself.

The rest of that night is a blank. My brain protected me. I've tried to recall it, but it's gone.

The next clear memory: the surgeon's office. I took notes because back then we didn't have home computers and I didn't want to miss a thing. I kept glancing at his shoes, thinking, Do I really want this Randy Travis doppelgänger in Gucci loafers cutting me open?

I was given a list of doctors. After a while, all the offices blurred together—white walls, stainless steel cabinets, crinkly paper gowns. Every time: "Make sure it opens in the front." As if the gown mattered when everything else was falling apart.

When the female plastic surgeon told me I had beautiful breasts, I broke down sobbing in her arms. It was the cruelest compliment—beauty tied to what I was about to lose. I sobbed because I didn't want beauty, I wanted to live.

During my Radiation Therapy consultation, I told the physician I wasn't thrilled with my surgeon. She gave me a piece of paper with a phone number. "Call this number," she said.

I did. I met with a new surgeon who told me he'd have to check with his partners. I sat there thinking:

Don't I have the right to change my mind about who cuts me open?

***

The Wednesday before Thanksgiving, my phone rang. The new surgeon told me his partners approved. I was on the OR schedule for December 3: lumpectomy and axillary node dissection.

I said yes.

I had been given the gift of cancer for my birthday. Now I had a new gift: a great surgeon and a date to wipe cancer off the slate. But the timing couldn't have been worse—my mother was flying in for Thanksgiving, and I had to pick her up at the airport.

What I really wanted to do was lace up my red running shoes and just run. But the detour sign was flashing: "Slow down. Cancer ahead." And I realized I was sentenced to wear as much pink as possible, right down to those running shoes. Pink was supposed to mean hope. To me, it meant a sentence. A color I never chose, painted on my body, my shoes, my life. Pink was not my color. Survival would have to be.

Chapter Six

Giving Up My Control

1993–1994

I had a surgery date. Thanksgiving was behind us, and the blur had begun. I was a cancer zombie—numb, half-present, dragging myself through motions like a puppet whose strings were tangled.

But I still had to work. So I called my manager. A major case had come up in Wichita: a million-dollar nightmare.

And in this one, it really was about a million-dollar baby.

Boxes of charts arrived at my house—something that would never happen today. My dining room table was piled high. I matched line items to patient records. Tedious? Yes. But it gave me something to do. It reminded me I still had worth.

At home, the mood darkened the minute Edward walked in. I'd clear the charts, make dinner, and after we ate, the cancer zombies crawled back into my head. Out spilled the fears.

My new Surgical/Oncology case manager invited me to a support group. I went, hoping for strength. Instead, I heard horror stories. I came home hysterical.

Edward picked up his glass of water and threw it in my face.

The shock was colder than the water itself. My skin stung, but my soul froze. That was love, Edward-style: drown the fire instead of hold it.

"My mother would do this to me when I was as upset as you are," he said.

I stood there stunned. "What happened to hugging me close?" I whispered. He shrugged and walked away.

Edward had deep mommy issues. Photos of Mary Alice covered a bedroom wall. One, in particular, haunts me still: a provocative 1930s shot. "Come hither" written all over it.

I once found her nightgowns in a linen closet. I stuffed them back quickly. But I never forgot.

The morning of December 3rd had a beautiful sunrise. I greeted it with a cup of tea in hand and walked out into the backyard with the cats to catch a glimpse of it before I went to surgery later that day.

After I showered and dressed, I drove to the mall to buy a new robe to wear while recovering. While I waited for Edward to come home, I popped a small bottle of sparkling wine and lit a fire. I toasted my breast like a fallen comrade—honoring its service, its beauty, its strength. For nourishing my babies, for comforting the dying, for every lover who had adored it. A ritual of goodbye in a glass of bubbles.

In pre-op, I told a little joke. Always leave them laughing.

Four hours later, I woke up in pain. Thank God for Fentanyl. I could sit up. Look around. No Edward. He was in the hall talking college football with my surgeon. It was always about Edward.

I was given a private room because I worked for the hospital system. A Demerol pump. Benadryl. No pain.

The next morning: drain instructions. Then we drove home—hitting every pothole. I had him pull over on a bridge so I could throw up.

I couldn't raise my arm. Couldn't cook. Couldn't do a damn thing.

We ate takeout. I did exercises in the shower. Gradually, I moved more.

At my post-op, two weeks later, I surprised my surgeon with stickers of birds perched on my incision. If my body had to be scarred, then damn it, I'd decorate it. I plastered stickers of birds on the incision, turning survival into art. He laughed until he cried. The drain came out. I was cleared to drive.

There was no Christmas at home that year. No tree, no lights, no comfort. Edward planned a trip to Germany instead—his version of festive.

I didn't have the strength to argue. I barely had the strength to pack. So I went. Not out of joy, but duty. I was no longer the heroine of my story—I was cast as an extra in Edward's.

Craig, his nephew, was wonderful. We visited Neuschwanstein, Oberammergau, charming towns covered in snow. Christmas Eve in Munich: the Christkindlmarkt.

Christmas morning: a train through the Alps to Interlaken. Snowflakes danced. At a cozy bed and breakfast, the owner, Greta, handed us wine and Swiss chocolates. Edward declined. I drank with her until I could smile again.

The next day, sunglasses in hand, we walked through fields of diamonds—sunlight sparkling on pure white snow. Unforgettable.

We moved on to Salzburg. The Sound of Music played in my head the entire time. The hills were alive, but I was not. My soundtrack clashed with the silence inside me.

Then home. The fairytale ended.

Chapter Seven

Blinders On and Running

1993–1994

I was running—faster than I realized—wearing blinders I didn't even know I had on. The cancer wasn't really behind me. Not yet. It would haunt me for years—through new beginnings, new homes, even new love. But I wasn't ready to see any of that. So I kept running.

There was no time to process. Radiation therapy started right after New Year's Day. Before Germany, they had already marked my breast—tiny blue dots, tattoos I hadn't asked for, reminders I didn't want.

Six weeks of the great unknown stretched ahead of me. Six weeks of driving to the hospital every morning like it was just another commute. Pretending. Pretending I wasn't terrified. Pretending this was normal. It wasn't.

I lay on a table while the linear accelerator was precisely aimed at my breast, then shot its beams into me. I clutched a small quartz crystal, a talisman in a sterile room. I told myself it held light, even while invisible fire burned me. What took forever to set up only took minutes to deliver. Then it was over. I got dressed. I walked out like it was nothing. Like I hadn't just been burned by invisible fire.

This wiped me out. I could be sitting at the dining room table auditing the chart, and before I knew it, my head would be on that table, and I'd be out cold. Exhaustion wasn't just a side effect — it was a thief. It stole my days, my work, even the simple act of holding my head up at the table. Eventually, my breast looked sunburned, but through it all, I knew I was a trouper.

Six weeks later, I was done. Goodbyes were said, and it hit me: for the first time in four months, no one was watching me. No one cared about me, no one was checking on me, and I was afraid. I was released to return to work and resume my life. What was my life? I thought I had reasonable control over it, but then the cancer zombies came, and my control was smashed to the ground. Everyone else controlled my life.

I flew back into Atlanta, rented a car, checked into my hotel, and was in the office by noon. I surprised all my coworkers, and we had a quick party planned for later that week over dinner. It felt great to be back. I had finished the million-dollar baby case as usual. Both hospitals could now bill for items that were not previously mentioned because the rule is that what is written in the chart indicates it happened.

Lexie had come to see me while I was undergoing radiation, and I had several work trips planned to Houston. Then Edward dropped a bomb on me. He told me that good friends of his had bought a house on an island in Florida and wanted us to see it. We took a quick weekend trip and came home with information on homes for sale, and Edward went ahead and bought two of them. I was stunned. This was a pattern for him that I could see; he was impulsive, and if his friends had something, he had to have something better.

He listed our home in Virginia, and life went on. This was what he did. He would want something, and he would get it.

The next strange thing he did was impulsively plan a solo trip to England. When I asked him why he was going, he told me that our friend Bertie would be with him, and he had been invited to visit an old girlfriend from when Edward attended college there. He packed and left. I had a bad feeling, I just didn't have proof.

Soon after he returned, a letter arrived from England, and he carelessly left it on his desk. I recognized the handwriting, I had seen it before, so I picked it up and read it. There was no doubt now that a dalliance had occurred.

That night at dinner, I brought it up. Calmly. I delivered my discovery quietly, my voice low. He didn't even flinch. Didn't look up from his plate. Betrayal served with dinner, swallowed without consequence.

He barely looked up from his plate. "It wasn't anything serious," he said. "You don't have to worry about it. I'll never see her again."

I sat there, stupefied. And just like that, the door slammed shut. He gave me no space to respond. No oxygen for my questions. No room for my hurt. So I said nothing. I couldn't afford the risk of saying more.

Edward was very good at shutting people down. It was the attorney gene—in him, and in his brother. He didn't argue quietly. He raised his voice. Always. Volume was part of the strategy. Overwhelm. Intimidate. Win.

One day, he told me—pointedly, not gently—to give my car to my daughter. It wasn't a suggestion.

It was an order. The kind of command that doesn't leave space for a response. And in my silence, I handed away another piece of myself.

He had three cars. I drove his Honda after that. So technically, I wasn't without transportation. But it wasn't about practicality. It was about control.

And the attic? He told me to clear out anything I didn't want. Like we were moving. But we weren't. Not yet. Rather than escalate things, I decided there was no point in becoming a shrew about it.

So I called Lexie. I told her I could pack up the car with things she might need and drive it to Birmingham, Alabama. I'd leave it in a parking garage for her. I mailed her one set of keys and tucked the second set into a box of things I'd packed just for her. What had gone up into the attic now had a home.

But I didn't know who I was anymore.

Lexie flew in to pick everything up. I took a bus back to Atlanta, worked for a week, then came home. And just like that, I no longer had a car. I didn't say anything. I simply started driving the Honda. It was available. But I hadn't chosen it. And just like that, I had let go of one more part of my life.

It made sense. But it didn't make sense at all. Lexie needed the car. She needed the things I jam-packed into it. But more of me slipped away in the process.

I was learning—piece by piece—that sometimes we surrender not because we want to, but because we can't see another way.

That was my season: surrender disguised as practicality. Each choice looked reasonable on the surface. But underneath, more of me was slipping away. Until all that was left was the island waiting to swallow me.

Chapter Eight

Every Man is an Island

C ue the Jimmy Buffett music—the unofficial soundtrack of island life. Except this wasn't a vacation. This was our new reality, and reality had teeth.

The move was not easy. There was a moving van full of antiques—somewhere. The truck driver was somewhere on I-95, which is nowhere near where he needed to be. Worse yet, when he finally got to our home, the truck could not get out of our driveway. I just stayed indoors and unpacked.

Within the first week, the storms arrived—as if the island itself was warning me. Paradise doesn't come free. It comes with teeth. Tropical storm warnings were issued, and we had our first dose of the reality of living on an island, four miles out in the Gulf of Mexico. And now what?

We had a lovely home. We were on the other side of the road from the Gulf, and our water was Apalachicola Bay. We had a dock, perfect to launch a small boat into the water, and I would often find one of our three cats lazily lying in the sun, enjoying their lives. I was hoping behind the turmoil of it all that the island would bring peace and that I could trade my running shoes for flip-flops.

Right now though, it was vital to do some re-arranging of our home. We had a lower level that was enclosed, and we were storing unpacked goods in that room. Now these things had to be moved up-stairs to keep them safe from the possibility of flood-ing.

Our home had been built on tons of dirt to raise it above sea level as much as county engineers would allow, and we learned through Tropical Storm Alber-to that we were fortunate to have this extra height.

We only had wet ground, and 24 hours later, puddles. There is an advantage to living on sand—the water has a place to go.

I did a lot of heavy lifting to get us all moved in, and this was something I wasn't supposed to do after surgery. I hauled boxes I shouldn't have touched, punishing a body still healing. Soon my arm swelled, lymphedema tightening its grip like the island itself was reminding me: nothing here would be easy.

I left my traveling job and traded it in for selling real estate. I took the classes, passed the state exam and began to work at an agency on the island. Selling homes on the island became my escape—windows with water views, couples dreaming of seashell lives. I sold them paradise, all while drowning in my own storm. The money was good, I had friends in the office, and I had fun. But I still needed that break that was coming soon because my life got turned upside down with the move, the career change and the storms.

In an attempt to make me feel better about everything that had just gone awry in my life, Edward planned a cruise on the Danube. He told me to pack for glorious evenings filled with excitement and day trips into cities renowned for their history and glamour. He told me he was doing this for me, as my family is from Budapest and we would be in Budapest for four days before cruising up the Danube.

I admit I was very excited to make this trip when he planned it. He was wise enough to know that he needed to make up for his misdeeds and the ill excuses over them, and I was determined to make it an incredible adventure. We both needed this escape, though for different reasons.

He was right—it was an unforgettable journey, one that made my soul hum with a kind of joy only deep roots could bring. I was *home,* and every corner of Budapest seemed to welcome me like a long-lost memory. We dined under the stars at the restaurant I had insisted on, and as the evening unfolded, I knew I had made the right choice. The food, the ambiance, the city wrapped in the glow of the night—it was everything I had imagined.

We wandered through the city, tracing the footsteps of history. We stood before the Roman ruins, now encased in protective glass, their timeless strength a reminder of the layers of life that built this place. And we ventured up the hill to Matthias Church, where the breathtaking views of the Parliament building stood as a proud sentinel along the river. From that height, it felt as though the whole city was unfolding beneath me, a living tapestry of history and homecoming.

It was there that Edward dropped to one knee and asked me to marry him.

Every cell in me screamed no. But fear is louder than desire. Fear of rage, fear of abandonment, fear of being left adrift. So I said yes—because sometimes survival sounds exactly like surrender.

We partied into the night.

Then the cruise departed, and we were off to Melk Abbey, a 900-year-old marvel at the top of a hill, and it was a climb. I could have wandered the abbey for more than an afternoon. It is a Baroque structure perched on that hill overlooking the Danube Valley, and it was peaceful and spiritual.

Overnight, we cruised into Vienna, where we had two days to explore to our hearts' content. I remember stopping to look into bakery windows and seeing deliciousness looking back at me.

It was a wonderful cruise that ended with me wearing an engagement ring that was heavy on my finger, not because of the diamond and filigree, but because it was his mother's engagement ring. That ring wasn't just heavy, it was haunted. His mother's presence sat between us, smiling like she'd won. Some ghosts don't rattle chains. They sit politely beside you, sipping tea, owning the room.

I told myself it would all be different this time—that the island, the new house, the engagement, the fresh start would somehow wash away the cracks I could no longer ignore. But deep down, even as I crossed the bridge onto that island, I knew: the island wasn't refuge, it was another cage. I was still running. And the blinders were still on.

Chapter Nine

Tides of Change

The Wedding Plans

I kept moving, because standing still meant drowning. Wedding plans began—not as a dream, but as another tide pulling me under.

But even the idea of the wedding felt like a trap. The satin wasn't fabric, it was suffocation. The ring wasn't love, it was a shackle. Even the vows tasted like saltwater in my throat. Every time I touched the fabric of the dress, every time I thought about the ring or the vows, I felt a new wave of nausea. It was like trying to hold my breath in an ocean that kept pulling me under.

Edward had planned the whole thing—where, when, who would be there—and it made my skin crawl. I couldn't even think about it without feeling suffocated, like there was no room for me to breathe.

I told myself I should feel joy. Isn't that what brides do? They gush, they glow, they count down days. But I wasn't glowing. I was gasping. This wasn't about us—it was about him. It was about control. It always was.

It wasn't a wedding. It was a contract. A transaction signed in silence, sealed in fear. A bargain I never wanted to make. I wasn't in love with the idea of marrying him; I was in love with the idea of escape. I was tired of running from my own thoughts, from his outbursts, from this man who would never give me the peace I needed.

But I stayed. I said yes.

I said yes the way a hostage nods when the gun presses harder. Not out of love. Out of survival. Saying no meant facing his rage, his sharp tongue, his lack of care. Saying yes meant at least I could survive the moment, keep things quiet, keep the storm from breaking out.

And so, I kept moving through the motions. I picked out flowers I didn't care about, a venue I didn't love, and I smiled because that was easier than explaining the panic I felt deep inside me.

The island was supposed to be my fresh start, but here I was, still running, still keeping my head down. The wedding plans were just one more way I was losing control, one more thing I didn't get to decide for myself.

The more I clawed at pieces of myself, the more they scattered like sand through my fingers. But I wasn't ready to admit it. Not yet. Running was still easier than reckoning.

Chapter Ten

Going to the Chapel

We were married in February, on the back steps of our island home. It was small, simple, and teal. Teal. Not white. Not ivory. Not mine. Teal because Edward said so. A dress I didn't choose, a color that shouted his control before I even said the words "I do."

Good friends—mine—helped make the house wedding magical. Some of Edward's people came too, including a friend who served as Justice of the Peace. My oldest son arrived early, bringing along his entire doo-wop music collection. That's how I ended up coming down the steps to "Going to the Chapel," and somewhere between the first note and the last step, the separation had already begun.

The friends who were supposed to perform the ceremony were hours late. No cell phones back then. No easy check-ins. Edward unraveled. He paced, barked into the phone, yelled like a man unhinged.

I said the wrong thing. I don't remember what it was. It doesn't matter.

The slap came like lightning: sudden, searing, impossible to take back. It cracked the air, cracked me. One moment, a bride. The next, a warning.

And still, the day went on. I put on the teal dress like armor that didn't protect me. I walked down the steps, every footfall heavier than the last. And I said I do, though every part of me whispered I don't.

I should've won an Oscar for best performance in a tragedy. Smiling, laughing, pretending, while my cheek still burned. I played the part so well, I almost fooled myself.

Edward, ever the showman, tossed pink T-shirts into the crowd like confetti at a circus. Pink—the color I already despised, now mocking me from the hands of my guests. My guests—my people—had flown in from all over. They brought no gimmicks. Just presence. Just love.

I know what you might be thinking. Why didn't I run? Why did I marry him?

Because I had nowhere else to go. Nowhere safe to land. Not yet. Survival doesn't always look like running. Sometimes, it looks like standing still in teal.

Chapter Eleven

The Honeymoon

(Sort Of)

We didn't take our honeymoon until May. There were reasons—I'm sure there were—but I don't remember them now. Probably cheaper airfare. Probably practicality. It didn't really matter.

Our honeymoon began like our marriage—divided. Two airlines, two flights, two separate seats in the sky. Together, but already apart. He booked a dingy little bed and breakfast—charming in theory, but tired and cheap in reality. The kind of place that made me feel like an afterthought. I went along with it, the way I went along with so many things.

In Bermuda, there aren't many cars. Mopeds are the way people get around. Of course, he rented one. He insisted on driving—he always had to be in control.

On the third day, his control literally tossed me aside. One sharp turn, and I was airborne—crashing into Bermuda's pink sand like a discarded rag doll. I got up—shaken, scraped, furious. But as I brushed myself off and looked out over the turquoise waters, I felt something loosen. The sea, the sky, the stillness—they reminded me that there were bigger things than him, bigger things than this moment. I made him drive me straight to the rental place. And I got my own moped.

From that moment on, I reclaimed something. My own handlebars, my own road, my own pace. Separate mopeds, separate lives, but for once, I chose. We explored the island, saw every scenic point, every attraction, even shopping. There were moments that almost felt like what honeymoons are supposed to feel like. It didn't erase the fall, though. It didn't change what I already knew somewhere deep down. But for a little while, it was good. And sometimes, good is enough when you're still hoping for the best.

Winter arrived—not that winter where there was snow and ice, but there were times when the bananas would freeze alongside the porch or some beautiful tropical plant would take a hit.

One afternoon, Edward came home with a friend for Hokie. A client had come in to see him regarding a legal matter and, with him, was a white sulfur cockatoo. He had smuggled the bird into the country. He didn't know what to do with Boris, the bird, and he had heard we had birds, so he arranged a meeting with Edward to give him the bird.

You don't just pop a new bird into a cage with your other bird, so we had to devise a safe place for Boris until he and Hokie could cohabitate. It didn't take long, and now I had two big birds plus that horrid biting lovebird to take care of and clean up after. Boris damn near had the big one when he bit through the coffee maker cord. It was time for him to live with Hokie. Two screeching birds and a screeching husband—what a scene in life. On top of this, Fish and Wildlife could take Boris if it was ever reported that he did not have a silver band on his leg.

One day, a client came into Edward's office and spun a tale of just knowing he should be awarded some land in the Bahamas. It was a family squabble about an inheritance, and Edward would have to go to the Bahamas to get records and see if this man had any rights to an inheritance.

Edward asked me to go too, and the only reason I said I would was because he would be busy all day researching records and I would be free to roam at my will. Just like that, he was gone in the morning and returned for dinner. The hotel was actually lovely. It was right on the water and the cruise ship channel was very close. I could sit in the shade and watch all the families having fun, and dream. I was dreaming when I heard the screaming start. I looked and saw a man with a bloody T-shirt. I ran to him to assess what had happened only to find out while he was closing the beach chair, the chair had snapped, catching his hand and cutting his finger off. I was looking for the finger, yelling for a bucket of ice and an ambulance. It did not dawn on me this was an island, a tourist island, and finding his finger, putting it on ice, and getting him to an ER on time wasn't going to happen. It wasn't dinner-time conversation. Besides, I did not feel like sharing it with Edward as he would not have shown any empathy at all.

Soon it was time to leave the island. Edward had one more document to copy, and I packed to leave. I stored our bags with the bell service and went to sit on the beach one more time. I was sitting quite peacefully, going over all the fun I had experienced there when there was screaming, lots of screaming. A woman sitting up by the pool was screaming and waving her arms. I could finally understand her. She was telling us her daughter was out in the water in a floatie of some sort and the water was taking her daughter out into the cruise ship channel about a quarter mile from shore.

I handed my purse and my shoes to a security officer, and I took off running. I untied my sundress and got out of it, and there I was in my underwear heading into the water. One minute I was daydreaming in the sun, the next I was stripping down to my underwear and running into the surf. Purse, shoes, sundress abandoned. Instinct took over. Another man joined me, and we could walk as the water was shallow. The child could see us coming, and when the water got deeper, we swam. We reached her and brought her back into her waiting mother, and while the hotel couldn't say it, I did. I unleashed on her about not watching her child. This is when Edward arrived. His first words weren't awe or gratitude. They were orders. Cover her. Control her. Contain her. He ordered security to wrap a towel around me as I was wet and almost naked, and he railed on the mother too.

I was able to change clothes in the bathroom as I had clean clothes in my suitcase. I tied my hair back, bought a hat in the hotel gift shop, and a pair of sandals. Security brought my purse, and Edward never said another word.

From the Bahamas, we flew into Miami for a few days before heading home. I thought it would be uneventful—sun, food, a hotel room before the drive back. But Miami had other plans. And what happened there still haunts me.

Edward had asked me to drive. Of course he had. Said the motion helped him sleep. So I drove, weaving through the maze of Miami with no GPS, no co-pilot, just the heat and a vague recollection of where our hotel might be. When I saw the sign for Miami Heat Arena, I thought I was close.

I exited the expressway and immediately felt it—off. A wrongness in the air. A group of older men sat playing cards under the overpass, shaded and still. This wasn't the place. This wasn't the turn.

I should've broken the law. I should've spun the wheel and fled. Instead, I followed the rules. And the rules almost killed me.

I made another turn. Mistake number two. I figured a few more rights and I'd be back on track. Behind me was a transport van shuttling elderly folks. The driver kept waving me to pass him, urgently, repeatedly—but I held back, afraid an elderly person might step out in front. I didn't know he was trying to get me out of there.

Relief came at a traffic light. I stopped, leaving space between my car and the one ahead—training I remembered. Just enough room to run. Then it happened.

A boy on a bicycle leaned onto my hood, pressing down like a seal. A thud slammed into the back of the car. Edward jolted awake. "What the hell was that?" Before I could answer, glass exploded inward. A gun barrel appeared, black and merciless, aimed at my head. The boy was the decoy. The camera bag was the prize. And my life was collateral.

Edward and the gunman locked in a silent tug-of-war over that damn bag. The weapon wavered between us, wild, erratic. I remembered the three-second rule. That's what I had. Not for Edward, not for the boy, but for me. Three seconds to survive.

I slammed the gas. The car lurched forward, knocking the boy off his bike. I swerved around the car in front, heading for the only thing I could trust—noise, pawnshops, people. Where there were pawnshops, there were police.

I screeched to a stop in a rougher part of town, heart pounding, sobbing uncontrollably. A crowd gathered. I didn't know if I could trust them. I could barely breathe. Then I saw it. Across the street, a police station. I climbed its steps shaking like a leaf in a storm.

Inside, I collapsed. The desk sergeant called for backup. Gave me water. Asked if I was hurt. "No," I sobbed. "But I ran someone over, about nine blocks back." A detective appeared. No one asked my name, no license, nothing. Just, "Come with me. We're going back in."

We drove through streets lined with cars more expensive than the homes they guarded. "Drug money," he said. "We want the big fish, not the guppies." At the scene, glass still glittered on the pavement. The camera bag strap lay in the street. Edward, ever helpful, jumped out to retrieve it.

The detective pointed out faces, named the prisons they'd come from. Told me they all knew he was a cop, and the last thing they wanted was a dead one. Then he looked at me almost casually and said, "You're one very lucky woman. Last week, they not only took her purse. They took her life."

Miami wasn't just heat and palm trees. It was survival. And I had survived—by three seconds. That night, I lay awake in our hotel bed, realizing how close I had come.

When we finally drove home, the silence between us was heavy. Edward never told the story. He couldn't—it wasn't about him. But I carried it inside me, the gun, the boy, the three seconds that changed everything. Home was supposed to be safe, but even there, I knew: survival doesn't always mean peace. Sometimes, it just means you made it back.

Chapter Twelve

The Lockout

We came home from Miami like two people living in different stories.

He was irritated, restless. The kind of man who couldn't sit in stillness without feeling the panic of his own irrelevance. He hadn't found the treasure he'd gone looking for—not in old family trees, not in the islands, not in me.

But I had found something. I'd found that I could show up.

I could fix things. I could be the one who saved the day, twice. And I liked how that felt.

No medals. No applause. But it stuck with me, like salt air in my hair. Something in me shifted out there on the water, and the moment we stepped back onto Florida soil, I knew—without needing to say a word—that something was about to end.

But I also carried something else home. The boy on the bike. The barrel of the gun. The three seconds that could have ended me.

I didn't have a name for it then. Now I know it was PTSD.

Every slam of a door, every unexpected shadow, every silence too long—it took me right back to Miami. Back to that hood, that gun, that breathless choice to hit the gas.

So while Edward stewed in his dissatisfaction, I was living with a different fire—the kind you can't put out, only contain. The kind that whispers *you survived, but you're not the same.*

I didn't lock the door behind him. I didn't pack a bag.

I just... started closing off the parts of me he used to walk through. Quietly. Like the wind.

He didn't notice the shift.

Men like Edward rarely do. They're too busy looking in mirrors to see what's happening behind them.

But I had already begun the quiet work of leaving. Not with suitcases—not yet. But in the way my voice stopped rising to meet his. In the way I stopped offering softness where it wouldn't be honored.

I wasn't angry. Not yet. Just tired. Exhaustion is its own kind of freedom.

He started talking about Costa Rica like it was the next shiny thing. Like moving to another country would fix what he refused to face in the mirror.

I nodded. I smiled in all the right places. But inside, I was doing the math.

What would it take to start over again? How long would I have to play the game this time? Could I survive one more fresh start that wasn't mine?

I was already gone, and he hadn't noticed.

That's the thing about emotional lockouts. You don't need a key.

You just stop letting them in.

Chapter Thirteen

Costa Rica or Bust

It was the summer of 1996, and we were headed to Costa Rica. Not for a vacation—though that's what everyone assumed. No, this wasn't about rest. This was about reinvention. About Edward trying to outrun his own ego again, chasing a bigger life like it might finally make him feel like enough.

For me? It was a maybe. A possibility. A place where I could breathe—if only a little. After Miami, after the boy on the bike and the gun at my head, I was still jumpy, still scanning shadows. Costa Rica wasn't just another move. It was me hoping the jungle, the ocean, the sheer distance could quiet the noise inside me.

I didn't know if it would be a beginning or an end. But I was willing to go, because staying wasn't an option anymore.

We landed in San José and were met at the airport by Maggie, an American real estate agent Edward had already connected with. I hadn't been included in the planning—not in the list of towns to visit, not in the price range, not even in the kind of property he thought we should buy.

I would've chosen something near the water. He chose the suburbs. Of course he did.

She took us to see homes that afternoon. Edward acted interested—charming, even. But I knew him well enough to recognize the signs. He wasn't looking for a house. He was looking for control, for image, for another way to keep himself at the center of the story.

And me? I was looking for a doorway.

The house he liked was in Escazú, tucked behind a gate with a handful of other homes. Gated communities were common there, and this one had its own strange kind of charm. The neighbors were all connected—family, mostly. A doctor. A hotel manager. Someone who ran boat tours. It looked safe, picturesque. It looked like something.

Inside, the house was spacious and beautifully built. Two living rooms, a butler's pantry, maid's quarters, hot tub, enclosed porch. There was even a guest house tucked on the grounds.

That guest house lit a spark in me.

Costa Rica was becoming a popular destination for people seeking affordable plastic surgery and recovery in private. I had a vision—a recovery house for women post-op. Quiet, restorative, healing. A business that gave me back something of my own.

For a brief moment, Edward seemed on board. He nodded. He asked questions. He didn't shut me down. I began to believe it might happen.

Contracts to purchase this house were drawn up. We met with a local attorney. Edward made calls back to the States, putting three properties up for sale and deciding we'd hold onto the lot that was still in my name. He had plans. He had money. He didn't pause to think. He never did.

But I was already watching the foundation crack. And I knew what came next.

When we got back to Florida, the shine wore off quickly. People were surprised.

An international move? To Costa Rica?

I brushed it off with practiced smiles and vague confidence, telling my family it would be fine. That I believed in the plan.

They didn't know the truth. They didn't know I was married to a narcissist with a God complex, a man who turned charm into a weapon and love into a leash. They didn't know how careful I'd learned to be. How quiet. How I'd memorized the trigger points in his moods and tiptoed through days trying not to set him off.

By then, I wasn't a wife. I was a handler.

Then came the moment I still laugh about—but not for the right reasons. Edward, of all people, was asked to run domestic violence meetings in the county. Yes, really. I almost spit out my vodka when he told me.

He, the man who belittled and bullied behind closed doors—was now being invited to lead conversations on healing. On safety. On survival. The absurdity would've been funny if it hadn't been so sickening.

While he played savior in public, I started going out with friends. I needed air. I needed witnesses. I needed someone—anyone—to see me.

***

One night, I sat alone in a dimly lit restaurant, when a man approached me with a look that told me he wasn't here for small talk. He leaned in, his voice low, and asked if we could speak privately. My pulse quickened as we stepped out onto the deck, the soft hum of the city fading as the boats rocked gently beneath the string lights and the glow of the moon.

He pointed to one of the boats, his eyes never leaving mine, and said, "I'm sailing to the Bahamas tomorrow. Come with me."

For a flicker of a second, the world paused. The invitation hung in the air, seductive and wild, tempting me to step into the unknown. I didn't go. But God, did I want to. And sometimes, wanting to? That's when you know you're already halfway there.

Back at home, things were fraying.

Edward had one of his infamous meltdowns—this time at my real estate office. I wasn't even there, but he made enough of a scene to get thrown out. Days later, when I went to pick up work I'd left behind, I found myself locked out.

Literally. My broker had changed the locks. And I knew right then—I was gone too.

What she didn't know was that I had two deals pending.

I called in a favor from a friend who worked there. I got in to my old office. I pulled my files. And walked those deals right over to a broker who let me run them through without taking a dime.

That money went straight into my savings account. It wasn't a windfall. But it was enough. It was mine. And I was ready.

We started to settle in.

I spent time learning Spanish from our gardener and our housekeeper. She cooked for us twice a week—her black bean soup was so delicious it tasted like comfort poured straight from the land.

We met the neighbors. We took Spanish lessons. I cleaned the guest house. And I made a business plan—one I believed in. I was going to bring plastic surgery patients down to recover in paradise. It felt bold. Smart. Mine.

Costa Rica was, without a doubt, the most beautiful place I had ever lived.

We stopped at roadside rotisserie stands once a week for chicken roasted over coffee wood. I learned to love ceviche. We took tours across the country. I swam in the Pacific. I went fishing. We walked through jungles and wandered weekend towns with names that sounded like poetry.

There were howler monkeys in the trees. There were horses on the beach. It was idyllic.

But even in paradise, shadows followed me. Miami lived in my body—startle responses, racing heart, nights of waking in a sweat. The scenery was new. The fear was old.

Then one day, Edward told me Katherine and his godson Michael were coming to visit.

Chapter Fourteen

And Then the Clock Ran Out

It didn't happen overnight. There was no sudden explosion. It built slowly, quietly, filled with poison, until I was backed so far into a corner that fear itself struck the match. And everything burned.

The arrival of his houseguests appeared to go smoothly on the surface. Polite smiles. Soft laughter. They toured the grounds, unpacked in the guest house, and made dinner plans.

Michael played with the birds. Kathrine and I sipped wine. But you could've sliced the tension between us with a knife.

I kept wondering what he'd told her. Did she know things had started to shift? That the cracks were forming? Did she know how restless he'd become lately—like Costa Rica had stopped being an escape and started feeling like a cage?

That debutante smile—cool, polished, practiced—never wavered. It said without words: *I know he loves me more.* There was sugar on the surface, but rot underneath.

And I felt it—the dread, the knowing: this week would not end well.

They went sightseeing most days—Edward, Kathryn, and Michael. I stayed home. That was my choice.

I had no interest in tagging along or pretending. I enjoyed the stillness, the space, the brief solitude. Let them tour waterfalls. I had laundry to fold, birds to listen to, a business plan still taking shape in my mind.

Kathryn was polite. Gracious, even. Michael was curious and sweet. But underneath it all, there was an edge—a current running between her and Edward that didn't need words. He was relaxed around her in a way I hadn't seen in a while.

It wasn't threatening. It was just... telling.

The house didn't feel invaded. But something had shifted. I could feel it. And I knew it was only a matter of time.

Then came the beach day.

We weren't staying overnight—Edward didn't want to pay for two hotel rooms. Typical. I brought a book I'd been saving: *The Mists of Avalon,* signed by Marion Zimmer Bradley herself. A little piece of my old life.

Kathryn and Michael went shelling. Edward barely acknowledged me.

"My book's on the blanket," I told him.

He shrugged me off.

We walked the shore. It was the first time in days I felt my shoulders drop, my breath steady.

But when we came back, my book was soaked. The tide had come in. The pages were ruined. It wasn't just a book. It was the last untarnished piece of who I used to be. And now even that was gone.

I told him I was upset. He deflected like always. "You should've locked it in the car," he snapped. As if my grief was foolish.

The car ride home was ice.

We showered. We dressed.

When he asked what was for dinner, I shot back, "Reservations."

His face twisted. But he swallowed whatever venom he wanted to spit.

Later that night, after the house was quiet, he came for me.

I was undressing when his voice—sharp, cold, accusing—cut through the silence: "Why are you so unfriendly to Kathryn? She's noticed. She's concerned."

I don't remember every word after that.

I remember yelling. I remember his face contorting into something twisted and unfamiliar. I remember the sound of my own heartbeat pounding like a drum in my ears.

And then—he lunged.

He shoved me hard against the dresser. My back hit the wood, the edge cutting into my spine. I couldn't move. I couldn't breathe.

Then, he grabbed one of our bed pillows and slammed it over my face.

The fear was instant. Blinding.

I fought. I kicked. My lungs screamed for air. I was crying, sobbing—muffled under the weight of that pillow. My hands clawed at his arms—useless against his strength.

The edges of the world blurred. The room tilted. I thought—*This is how I die. Right here. Right now.*

Desperation took over. I reached behind me, my fingers searching, frantic, and they landed on cold glass.

The lamp. Heavy. Solid. I swung with everything I had. The impact sent him stumbling. The pillow dropped. The lamp shattered—glass everywhere, glittering across the comforter I'd once thought was beautiful.

I gasped—ragged, choking—then I ran. "Come near me," I shouted, my voice shaking, "and I'll call the police." I bolted to the maid's quarters, shoved the dresser against the door, locked myself in.

And I sat there. Alone. My whole body trembling. The taste of fear in my mouth. The room spinning. And in that moment, I knew the match had been struck. And nothing—nothing—would ever be the same.

Yet I made breakfast the next morning. Moved through the motions like nothing had happened. But inside, my wheels were spinning. Not with rage. Not with panic. With calculation. I was starting to see things for what they were—stripped of excuses, stripped of charm. Every smile felt sharper. Every silence, louder.

Something had shifted. And I wasn't going to unsee it.

They decided to go sightseeing. I said I'd stay home, offered a polite smile. Kept my voice even. Steady. Practiced.

As soon as the car pulled out of the driveway and the electronic gate began to close behind them, I moved.

I picked up the phone and called Maggie. My hands shook. My voice was flat.

"Can you come get me?"

She didn't ask questions. She didn't need to.

When she arrived, I was already waiting—bag packed, bruises darkening into the unmistakable shape of handprints. I didn't have to explain. The bruises said everything.

We drove straight to the emergency room. I wanted a police report. Documentation. Something official. Something real—because I still wasn't sure I believed it myself.

Afterward, Maggie brought me back home. Waited while I packed. Again. I scooped up my cat, Miss Scarlett, and we were gone.

We stayed at Maggie's until things simmered down—until some kind of sense could be made from the wreckage.

When Edward, Kathryn, and Michael came back, they returned to an empty house and a note that read:

> **Do NOT try to find me. I filed a police report.**

Over the next several days, Edward was allowed to speak to me only through our attorney, Roger. Everything went through him—no direct contact.

We negotiated the terms: what was mine, what I had brought into the marriage, what I would be taking home.

Roger arranged a moving company. He stayed in the house with me while my things were packed and prepped for customs. I set up a storage unit and left instructions for delivery once I had a new address.

Edward behaved himself. He was embarrassed. Humiliated, I think, that Roger had to witness it all.

I thought I finally had everything. We left.

Edward bought my plane ticket home—something he always said he'd do if I ever changed my mind.

My mind had been changed the night he tried to kill me.

At the time, I refused to sign over the car. I told Roger I needed to think about it.

That was the one loose thread still dangling. And then Roger took me back to Maggie's.

Chapter Fifteen

Whispers of the Foreboding

I woke before dawn in Maggie's guest room, my heart pounding in the stillness. Outside, the police cruiser sat idling beneath the streetlight, the engine a low hum against the quiet.

They were there for me. Watching. Just in case. I was supposed to feel safe. But I didn't.

The bruises on my arms hadn't faded. The panic still skittered under my skin. And yet—I had to face him one more time. There were things left to handle. Loose threads that wouldn't tie themselves.

The car was one of them.

We had an appointment that day at the attorney's office to sign over the car. Just a few more hours and I'd be free. I told myself that like a mantra.

But before the appointment, somehow, I ended up in the car with him. I can't even tell you how exactly. Maybe it was logistics. Maybe it was convenience. Maybe it was one last twisted act of false civility. I only know I sat there, stiff and silent as he drove, every nerve in my body screaming.

And then—because life loves its cruel sense of humor—the car started acting up. The engine sputtered. He cursed under his breath. I barely spoke.

We pulled into a McDonald's parking lot—of all places—while he messed with the car. I sat there, thinking over and over: *This is the last time. The very last time.*

We both got out of the car, and I asked—exasperated—"You didn't take the car in?"
That was all it took. His voice rose, sharp and venomous, until everyone in the parking lot was staring

His voice rose, sharp and venomous, until everyone in the parking lot was staring at us. His fists clenched, his face twisted, and then he screamed:

"You CUNT!"

That was it. I leapt to my feet and I ran.

Not a few steps. Not across the lot. I ran like hell itself was at my heels.

My sandals slapped the pavement. The heat rose up in waves off the asphalt, thick and heavy in my lungs. My heart was a jackhammer, my breath ragged, my arms pumping like I could outpace death itself.

Block after block blurred past. McDonald's, strip malls, strangers staring. I didn't look back. I couldn't. I only knew one thing: keep going. If I stopped, if I hesitated, I was done.

By the time Roger's office came into view, my body was drenched, my hair sticking to my face, my legs quaking—but I didn't stop until I slammed through those doors, chest heaving, and gasped, *"Call Maggie."*

Roger called. Maggie came. She drove me back to my house.

We pulled in through the gate, and I locked it behind her. We were loading her car when we heard it—the horn blaring on the private road. Screaming. It was Edward. Leaning on the horn. Yelling to anyone who could hear to "call the police" because he was "being robbed."

Maggie and I locked eyes. We both knew what this was. He had my car—parked it to block the driveway. We weren't leaving.

Maggie pulled out her phone to call the police. Then—crashing sounds. From the back wall of the house. I signaled her: "Start the car." I ran to the gate. There was my car. The driver's door hanging open.

I shoved the car down the road, watching as it rolled, faster and faster, until it crashed into the ditch with a metallic thud.

I stood there, breath heaving, heart pounding in my ears. Then I got into Maggie's car—and I laughed.

Not because it was funny. Nothing about it was funny. I laughed because my nerves were shot, my hands were shaking, and somehow I knew my car was damaged.

Of course it was. Everything was damaged.

We left.

Chapter Sixteen

The Leaving

Walking Away in 1996

I didn't get the kind of ending you see in movies. There was no dramatic slam of a door, no tears on cue, no tidy closure.

Instead, I spent the night curled in fear and fierce resolve at Maggie's house. A patrol car idled outside like a silent sentinel. I didn't sleep. I planned my escape.

At dawn, they came for me. My escort, a uniformed deputy, stood beside me, steady and silent, as I walked into the airport. He didn't leave my side at the counter or at the gate.

When it was time, I turned to Maggie, the kind of friend who doesn't flinch in chaos. She'd take care of Miss Scarlett now, my elegant, knowing cat who had watched the worst unfold with wide, patient eyes.

I hugged Maggie tightly. There were no promises. Just truth. And then I stepped through the doorway and out onto the tarmac.

The sky was split with morning light, un-apologetic, blazing, alive. And there it was: the staircase to the plane. I didn't glance back. Not this time.

Every step I climbed was a step away from fear. Every rise of my foot declared: *I am done running.* I didn't cower. I ascended. I climbed those stairs not as a victim, but as a woman on fire, and there was power in my stride.

I had freedom in my breath and a heartbeat louder than jet engines. This was the day I took my life back. The engines ignited. We were airborne. I was gone.

Hours later, I stepped off the plane in Detroit. My close friend, Judie, had sent her husband to greet me, and when I saw his face—steady, familiar, kind—I felt the tension in my chest finally begin to ease.

I was home. I was safe. And for the first time in what felt like forever, I could breathe.

I slept a lot. I slept without fear for the first time in years. I let my body heal slowly, while my mind tried to catch up.

Maggie mailed me the photographs she'd taken of my bruises—purple, green, fading but undeniable.

I remember holding those pictures and staring at them like they belonged to someone else.

They were proof. Evidence if I needed it. A story my body told, even when I couldn't find the words.

I knew I'd have to file for divorce eventually. I knew the fallout would come. But for now, I didn't have to—because for now, I was alive. And that was enough.

A few weeks later, I knew where I needed to be: Chicago. The city called to me. I needed to be somewhere I could live without a car, somewhere I could blend into the noise and the motion. I missed it all—the smells, the streets, the pulse of it.

I opened a bank account, moved into a second-floor apartment in an old brownstone, and for a while, I slept on a ratty old sofa bed someone had left behind.

That's when the memory of St. George Island came flooding back—my furniture, my things, the pieces of my life Edward was selling right along with the house.

I called an old friend. I booked a flight. I borrowed a truck, called a maintenance man I knew, and spun a sweet little lie about visiting and forgetting my keys. He met me there and changed the locks without question.

I hired a crew of oyster fishermen, and in a matter of hours, the house was emptied. I paid everyone generously, loaded the truck, and started the four-teen-hour drive back north.

And no—I didn't call Edward. I had no interest in hearing his voice ever again. But I did call Marilyn, the real estate agent. I caught up with her casually at first, and then I told her, "I'm in Chicago. I've left Edward."

She was quiet for a moment, then relieved. "I'm so glad you're alright," she said softly.

Then I told her the rest.

"I've been to the house on the island," I said. "And I emptied it out."

The silence on the other end was deafening. Finally, she asked, "Does Edward know?"

I said gently, "No. I can't tell him. The new keys are on the kitchen counter."

We hung up. And for a moment, I felt bad—bad that Marilyn would be the one to deliver the news.

But then I laughed. Because this time, when his rage exploded, he'd have no one to take it out on.

Not me. Not ever again.

For years, I thought running was the only way to survive. Running from men. From places. From the echoes of violence that never seemed to let me rest.

But in Chicago, something shifted. For the first time in decades, I wasn't running. I was standing still—just me, my scars, and a city that had always called me home.

The bruises would fade. The nightmares would linger. The story wasn't over.

But I had a beginning again. And this time, it belonged to me.

Chapter Seventeen

Haunted

L eaving didn't mean it was over. Not really. Edward tried to file a police report on me, but the authorities wouldn't touch it—out of state, out of reach. I breathed a little easier, but not much.

I found a job. I made new friends. I reconnected with old ones. I bought a Christmas tree for my new apartment. On the outside, it looked like life was moving forward. But inside? I was haunted.

I saw him everywhere. A shape on a street corner. A glimpse in a restaurant. A shadow at the grocery store.

I knew he could show up at any moment. I knew exactly what he was capable of. The bruises faded, but the fear didn't. The fear lived on—quiet, sharp, always just beneath the surface.

That's the part no one tells you about leaving: The paperwork gets filed. The bruises fade. But the fear? The fear stays.

I lived with it. Caller ID became my shield. Heavy locks lined my doors. I crossed streets at the slightest suspicion. My heart stopped every time I thought I saw him—standing under a streetlamp, waiting around a corner.

Still, I walked the city. I always had. Chicago was built for walking, and I wasn't going to give that up. I answered an ad to walk a dog in my neighborhood, and that's how I met Penny—a full-sized English Staffordshire with the sweetest eyes and a steel spine. Her owner gave me the code word: one syllable that turned Penny into a bodyguard. With that word in my pocket, I felt safe. Protected.

After passing the background check, I was given a key to the house. Every day, Penny and I walked. She'd nap at my apartment, I'd cook dinner, and when Jim called on his way home, she'd hop into his car. For a woman still living in fear, it was the perfect arrangement.

When Jim moved to the suburbs that spring, I cried saying goodbye to Penny—my unlikely protector.

By summer, the festivals came alive—food, music, laughter on every corner. My life *looked* normal again, or as close as I could manage. I returned to wound care, working with doctors and patients. Precision and focus kept my mind occupied. But the edges of the past were always there—shadows I couldn't outrun.

Back in Cleveland, my family was changing. My mother had been diagnosed with Alzheimer's. My sons were still there, my daughter was still in Texas. And I was the one who had run. They didn't understand. I didn't expect them to.

When I returned to Chicago, I moved into Marina Towers—those iconic round towers on the river. For the first time in years, I felt like I had carved out a piece of freedom. I'd look out over the city lights and tell myself: *this is mine.*

Through my breast cancer support group, I met Darcy—my steadfast friend for years to come. She nudged me toward a dating site. I was still technically married, but that felt like a technicality compared to the freedom I was starting to taste.

There were colorful dates, funny men, flashes of joy. But there were also process servers—waiting to corner me with papers I wasn't ready to face. I ducked them, avoided them, lived cautiously.

By winter, life began to soften. A new coat, warm boots, nights out with Darcy. One of those nights changed everything. We were out at a local spot when I met him—Larry. A stranger at first. Just a man with kind eyes, a voice that carried warmth.

We talked for hours, then exchanged numbers, then voices over long phone calls that felt like lifelines. Finally, we set a date. December, snowy and cold. I almost turned back that night. Fear whispered to me with every step past the House of Blues, across Clark Street. But I kept walking.

And the man I met that night—the man I later called Larry—was the one I finally ran *to*.

Chapter Eighteen

And There He Stood

I walked in with the weight of everything I'd been through clinging to me like damp clothes.

It was cold outside—colder than I expected for a night out in Chicago. I hadn't planned to stay long. Hell, I hadn't planned for anything.

But then I looked up... and there he was. Not glowing under a spotlight like in the movies. Just there. Sitting. Waiting. Real.

I paused—not from hesitation, but recognition. Something inside me whispered: *This is the moment. This is the turning.*

I didn't know I'd love him yet. But I knew I wasn't going to run.

I'd spent the afternoon debating what to wear. In the end, I chose sexy. Full throttle. A top that showed off my best assets. A mini skirt that showcased my legs—because let's be honest, my legs are phenomenal. Always have been. Always will be.

While everything else was changing, those legs? Damn near perfect.

Hair and makeup? Done.

Scent? Always Obsession by Calvin Klein—just enough that if we hugged, he might carry it home with him.

After four incredible phone calls, I had a strong suspicion we'd be hugging. And I was already working overtime to keep the hotter thoughts at bay.

I checked my coat, tossed my shoulders back, and walked—no, *strutted*—toward the back of the restaurant. I felt him watching me. Every step. Taking it all in.

God, it felt good.

After years of feeling invisible, dismissed, over-looked—I felt seen. Wanted. Like I was walking in slow motion and he was there to witness it.

We greeted. We laughed. I kissed him on the cheek. Then we sat down to dinner.

It lasted three hours. Eventually, the staff started giving us that *Are you leaving... or moving in?* look. So we left.

We walked hand in hand down State Street, taking in the Christmas windows at Marshall Field's. He held one of my hands. I'd forgotten my gloves, so I tucked the other into my coat pocket.

He walked me home. We shared that hug.

And I was in bed early. And I was happy.

Chapter Nineteen

A Clean Break

B y the end of January, the "L" word was in the air—heavy, undeniable, and simmering between us. By February, I had packed up and moved into his condo.

Yes, it was fast.

No, I wasn't rebounding. I'd been single for what felt like forever, a string of dates and half-finished stories behind me. I'd stitched myself back together, piece by piece, until I could stand tall again. But with him? With him, I didn't need to stitch anything.

The connection was electric, undeniable. The sex? Terrific. Every touch, every whisper between us felt like a pulse of raw energy—intimate, fiery, and as natural as breathing. When we were together, the world faded to just the two of us. The physical connection was more than just skin—it was everything. And the way he made me feel, made me *want*—it was something I hadn't known I was missing.

But this? This was different.

It was also time to finish what Edward had started—and dragged out. I contacted an attorney in Florida, laid it all out, and we got the ball rolling.

This time *he* would be the one served.

Edward had to prove his arrival and departure times in Tallahassee and—get this—he had to be escorted by sheriff's deputies across three county lines. That's right: Three counties. Three escorts. And a final handoff into Franklin County.

Meanwhile, I was tucked away in a gated community under watch by local patrol—because even now, safety wasn't guaranteed.

When the court date arrived, I had to pass through a brand-new metal detector at the courthouse—installed because of him. My leg bounced uncontrollably. My nerves were a mess. It was the first time I'd seen him since the day I shoved my car into a ditch and ran.

And then he strolled in like he owned the damn place.

The judge looked up, sighed, and said, "Mr. Lemay, you have the honor of being the reason I now have a metal detector in my courtroom."

I rolled my eyes so hard I nearly saw behind me.

Edward had once practiced law in this very county. He and the judge were on a first-name basis, which was gross—but oddly fitting. Then came the kicker—when asked why he'd let his hair grow out, Edward replied, "Your Honor, I can't afford a haircut."

Somewhere, Karma giggled.

The judge heard the case. Granted the civil divorce. And just like that, it was over. Edward was promptly escorted out and back through the counties like a toxic parade. I sat in my attorney's office, waiting.

Two hours later, the phone rang: Edward had boarded his flight. Was I relieved? Somewhat. But not completely. I just wanted the chapter closed.

The next morning, I flew back to Chicago. This time, I used the airport in Panama City instead of Tallahassee—just to be safe. I kept looking over my shoulder until the plane took off.

When I landed, Larry was there waiting—his arms, his presence, his warmth.

And I was home.

Chapter Twenty

At Last

We were in love. Not just the everyday, comfortable kind—But the kind that catches fire every morning. The kind that hides in small gestures, that makes you feel like you're falling for each other for the first time—again and again.

It was fresh. It was real. It was ours.

One night in late winter, over dinner at a cozy restaurant, I looked him in the eye and asked, "Can you see us married? Because if you can't, I'll be heartbroken."

No games. No pretense. Just truth—bare and brave.

Without missing a beat, he said, "Yes, I can."

Boom.

The air shifted. The future opened.

The real proposal came later that June, at his condo. We'd already had the talk.

But this time, he looked at me and said, "I'm not going to ask you again."

It wasn't a threat. It was a reminder—because he'd already asked, and I hadn't heard him.

I'd kept talking on and on, as I often did when I was nervous. Chatter was my shield, my tell. But he saw through it. God, he saw through me—and still, he stayed.

No more detours. No more doubt. We were doing this—together.

I was engaged to the best man I'd ever met.

Everyone around us saw it. They saw the love. They saw how we fit. They saw the magic.

And this time... I wasn't running.

Chapter Twenty-One

Epilogue

Why I Told It Now

It took me years to write this. Decades, really. Because healing isn't linear, and memory plays tricks. Because I had to survive it first. Then make sense of it. Then be brave enough to tell it out loud.

There were years I couldn't even say his name. Years I downplayed what happened. Years I told myself, *It's over, let it go,* but the truth still burned in my bones—and so did the knowledge that he was dangerous, unwell, unchecked.

This isn't just a story about leaving. It's about coming back to myself.

I wrote this book with a steady heart and shaking hands. Not for revenge. Not for pity. But to reclaim my story.

To show what it really looks like to live through abuse, to walk away, to start again, and still believe in love.

I wrote this because maybe you need to hear it—that you're not crazy, you're not weak, and you're sure as hell not alone.

This is my truth. And I'm standing in it now.

With fire. With grace. With no more hiding.

Author's Note

Dear Reader,

If you've made it here, thank you. Truly.
Writing this book was like pulling threads out of old
scars—painful, but necessary. Reading it might have
stirred up your own memories, your own questions,
your own ghosts.

If you are in a place of hurt, please know this:
you are not alone. You never were. There is help, there
are hands waiting to steady you, and there is a life
beyond the fear you might be carrying right now.

For those who want to take the next step, here are resources that can make a difference:

- **National Domestic Violence Hotline (U.S.):** 1-800-799-SAFE (7233) or text "START" to 88788

- **RAINN (Rape, Abuse & Incest National Network):** 1-800-656-HOPE (4673)

- **Local crisis centers** and **support groups** in your community—find them, lean on them, and let them remind you that healing is possible.

I tell my story not to dwell on the past, but to shine a light for others who are still walking through their own darkness. You deserve safety. You deserve freedom. You deserve love that doesn't hurt.

And if my words helped even one person believe that, then every painful memory I pulled onto the page was worth it.

With fire.
With grace.
And with gratitude,

Carole Sanek

HELD

Book Three Teaser

GWN Publishing, LLC

Our Wedding

July 1, 2000

Morning light spilled across our room, and there he was—coffee in hand, smile on his lips—just as he always did

.Larry sat on the edge of the bed, brushed the stray hair from my face, and for a moment, I forgot everything but him. The simple ritual of his love grounded me, even as butterflies bumped wild inside me. Today was the day. Our wedding day.

The dress hung waiting in the doorway, a promise wrapped in satin. Friends and family were already gathering at a nearby hotel, their laughter floating in through phone calls and quick visits. By noon, the ladies and I were in a salon, buzzing with anticipation. We laughed, we gossiped, we ate catered lunch between snips of scissors and swirls of hairspray. I watched joy ripple across their faces and thought: *this is what love builds—a circle that holds you up when you need it most.*

Larry had made me a headpiece by hand, lace and satin stitched together with tenderness. Holding it felt like holding a piece of his heart. Every thread whispered devotion. By late afternoon, the house filled again—makeup brushes sweeping across cheeks, voices echoing through the rooms. Larry teased that I never let him nap. He wasn't wrong.

At five, we left for the Community Center where we'd rented the lower level. Decorations bloomed. A borrowed archway framed the landing where we'd stand. On a nearby table, three cakes waited—one topped with strawberries, one classic white, one crowned with blueberries. Red, white, and blue for a holiday weekend, but to me, they looked like celebration itself.

And then—it was time.

I stood trembling at the base of the stairs as Sarah Brightman's *Unexpected Song* filled the air. My dearest friend and her daughter walked ahead of me, Michael Crawford's voice swelling into the wedding march. My breath caught. Could I even climb those steps?

Larry saw it in my eyes. He came down to meet me. He took my arm. And together, we walked up—through the arch, into the next chapter of our lives.

We wrote our own vows. Words stumbled and caught, but every line was true. Tears streamed down both our faces. And when the judge pronounced us husband and wife, applause rose, laughter followed, and the world shifted into something more whole.

The reception blurred into dancing, music, and joy. My best friend caught the bouquet, Larry playfully pulled the garter from my leg to cheers and laughter. We were surrounded, lifted, *held* by everyone we loved.

But the real moment came later. Quiet.

Just us.

After the crowd had gone, he unzipped my dress, kissing my shoulders as the fabric slipped to the floor. We knew each other's skin already, but this was different—deeper, more permanent. That night wasn't just about becoming man and wife.

It was about becoming something stronger.

Something unbreakable.

Held.

About the Author

Carole Sanek

 Carole Sanek is a life coach, podcaster, and author. Carole decided to create a series of memoirs based on a significant trauma in her life that turned her entire world upside down. She spent over forty years turning it right-side up again. Carole spends her time with her dog companion Rosie, walking in the mountains of North and South Carolina.